PROJECT SPONSORSHIP:

WINNING STRATEGIES
FOR EXECUTIVE LEADERS

PROJECT SPONSORSHIP:

WINNING STRATEGIES FOR EXECUTIVE LEADERS

BY

TERRI CARBONE

WITH SHEILA ASHDOWN

Copyright © 2013 by Terri Carbone

All rights reserved. No part of this book may be reproduced or transmitted in any form or by any means whatsoever without express written permission from the author, except in the case of brief quotations embodied in critical articles and reviews. Please refer all pertinent questions to the author at successfulprojectsponsorhip.com.

ISBN-13: 978-1494264567
ISBN-10: 1494264560

Cover Design
by
Joseph Loveria

Book Design
by
Suzanne Chiles
Fresh Ink Foundry

To Glenn, Julie and David.

May this book help others be
exceptional sponsors like yourselves.

CONTENTS

Preface ix

Introduction 1

Chapter 1
The Role of the Project Sponsor 8

Chapter 2
Communicating the Project Purpose 16

Chapter 3
Getting Specific with a Real Project Plan 22

Chapter 4
Managing Risk 33

Chapter 5
Project Status and Communication During Execution ... 41

Chapter 6
Achieving Operational Readiness 49

Chapter 7
Going Live…and Beyond 59

Chapter 8
Recognizing Your Team 70

Conclusion 75

Preface

For over twenty-five years, I've worked in project management and process improvement for major corporations. Time and again I've been brought in to deliver a quality project, on time and within budget. In multiple instances, I've served as project manager for companies that hadn't delivered on time in more than three or four years—until I showed up and turned things around. Major customers, who were ready to walk out, have been saved. It's because of this experience that I can provide you with the proven solutions that have made the difference.

I was inspired to write this book because, though there are thousands of books on project management and corporate leadership, rarely does anyone talk about the crucial role of the project sponsor. I wanted to remedy that. Even though project management is a certified profession with many excellent methodologies, at the end of the day, the best project manager is nothing without an equally great project sponsor. Over the course of my career, I've worked for bad sponsors. It's a fight to get the job done, and it's disappointing to watch a project go downhill and feel powerless to save it.

On the flip side, I've worked with great leaders, who armed themselves with critical questions, and who were not willing to compromise their responsibilities. These great sponsors backed up their teams, asked hard questions throughout the process, and supported the work through to the finish line. It's my goal to see more of those great sponsors.

I'm confident that this practical guide will improve the lives of project managers and project sponsors. My winning strategies will help you strengthen the bottom line of your projects, foster better relationships with your team members, and enhance your personal reputation as an executive.

Introduction

There Has to Be a Better Way…

Sam Smith has been the vice president of operations of a Fortune 500 company for going on ten years. It's been a good run, with lots of perks and successes. But the company is in the red after years of economic decline, and looking for much-needed ways to trim fat and bolster revenues. The accounts payable system is in serious need of an update. But it's going to cost upwards of a million dollars to replace, so the stakes are high, and morale is already spread thin around the office; people have been doing "more with less" for a couple years now, and they're burnt out. Not that anyone tells him that, of course; Sam can tell that no one wants to be the squeaky wheel and risk losing their job in this less-than-recovered economy. But Sam is no dummy—he can feel the bad vibes around the cubicles.

This new accounts payable system could be crucial to the company. If they could reduce their late fees and take advantage of vendor discounts for early payment, that would translate to a lot of savings. Not to mention that a better system would cut way down on the time that employees spend manning the phones, taking calls from vendors. It killed Sam to think about how much time and money was being thrown away. If only they could capture those savings and reinvest those funds elsewhere…

Better accounts payable technology would help with all of that. But it was a big undertaking, and the company's last few projects hadn't gone so well—way over budget, way past due. One of the best project managers in the company had thrown her hands up and quit after that last debacle. He couldn't blame her.

There had to be a better way.

...

Chances are, if you're reading this book, you may be able to relate to Sam Smith's dilemma. Like our friend Sam, most corporate executives are big thinkers who got to their position through ambition, forward-thinking, and a tolerance for taking risks. Not coincidentally, these three qualities are also what make for an effective business. Any company that wants to compete in their market, inspire loyalty in their employees and customers, and generate healthy revenue—they must grow, improve, and innovate. In practical measures, this growth happens by way of projects: short-term endeavors that are designed to accomplish a particular set of business goals, and which have a defined beginning and end, and specific deliverables and success criteria. "Project" is a seemingly simple term, but the success or failure of a project can make or break a company.

Unfortunately, although projects are often crucial to a company's success, too many projects fail. In fact, in a 2011 survey of 163 companies, PM Solutions found that the average firm spent $200 million per year on projects. And of that $200 million, 37 percent (or $74 million) was spent on troubled or failed projects.[1] Here's another perspective: According to

---

[1] PM Solutions, *Strategies for Project Recovery: A PM Solutions Research Report* (2011), http://www.pmsolutions.com/collateral/research/Strategies for Project Recovery 2011.pdf.

the Project Management Institute, when companies properly manage a project, they risk only $20 million per every $1 billion spent. Companies who mismanage their projects risk a whopping $280 million for every $1 billion.[2] The numbers are mind boggling.

What Does It Mean to "Fail," Exactly?

You might see those dire statistics and think, "Not my company!" Perhaps that's because the word "fail" is admittedly strong. It's a hot potato that no one wants to be left holding. And sure, project failure *can* be extreme—perhaps the project has to be abandoned completely; it loses substantial revenue for the company; or it negatively affects the company's stock price. Most often, though, project failure is a matter of degree:

- A project runs many months late, wasting time and money.

- A project is completed by deadline, but isn't fully realized, and is rolled out in a state of half-completion that leaves users frustrated for months, years, or longer.

- A project, or the change around it, is mismanaged, frustrating good employees and causing low morale and costly turnover.

- Mismanagement erodes the trust and respect that your employees or company hold for you.

Even if a project is a so-called success—which is too often defined simply as "it met its deadline"—its weaknesses can spell trouble for the overall success of the company. We've all

---

[2] Project Management Institute, *PMI's Pulse of the Profession: The High Cost of Low Performance* (March 2013), http://www.pmi.org/~/media/PDF/Business-Solutions/PMI-Pulse Report-2013Mar4.ashx.

seen too many news stories in recent years about companies that have laid off good employees, have frozen or cut pay and benefits, or have shut their doors completely. These are the very things that cut to the core of people's lives. The recession has not been kind to many, and companies have had to respond by becoming savvier and more agile than ever. They absolutely cannot afford to throw money into poor management. It harms the bottom line, it harms employees, and it ultimately erodes the loyalty of clients and customers.

Why Do Projects Fail?

There are many reasons a project can fail, and I'll be addressing them in this book. Reasons include:

- Unclear or unrealistic expectations
- Lack of leadership from project sponsors
- Inexperienced project managers
- Lack of project management protocols
- Inattention to risks
- Lack of planning
- Unrealistic schedules and deadlines
- Inadequate resources or skill sets

Who Can Benefit from This Book?

First and foremost, this is a book for executives who are acting as project sponsors. Whether you're taking on the role of project sponsor for the first time, or you're looking to improve the way projects are managed in your company, there is something for you in this book. However, I also hope that this book will be useful to project managers, to help them know where their job responsibilities end and the sponsor's begin.

A successful project depends very heavily on the mutually beneficial relationship between a project sponsor and a project manager. They should—and can!—have a great, trusting relationship that works in complement to create a successful project. Their roles must work together, as they each bring something of great value to a project. While the project manager is on the ground, managing the day-to-day details and monitoring the temperature of the project, the sponsor keeps an eye on the project's overall effect on the company. Project managers do not typically have employees under them, so they operate solely on the goodwill of the relationships they create with their co-workers, along with their ability to effectively communicate their needs to the sponsor.

Sponsors, on the other hand, are the "heavies." They have weight to throw around and can use that power to secure the resources, money, and support that the project manager needs. The sponsor has access to the ears of the stakeholders and other executives, and has the power to bring in resources when necessary.

Ultimately, if sponsors *and* project managers are better educated about their role in the project process, they can more effectively take advantage of the benefits of their partnership. So, I encourage you to share this book, and its very simple philosophies, with any member of your project team who you think can benefit from it.

How Will This Book Help You Lead Projects to Success?

By their very nature, projects always carry with them a chance of failure. Since all projects are future focused, all projects are risky. However, in my many years of experience, I have seen time and again that it's the commonsense strategies that are most effective in minimizing risks and maximizing both the efficiency and quality of a team's process and product. And when your team excels, so do you. When your team looks great, you look great.

This is not a project management how-to. There are plenty of great project management books on the market. My goal here is to give you, the project sponsor, a baseline understanding of the specific project-management documents and procedures you will encounter. If you know the purpose these documents and procedures serve, you can better assess their quality.

Project Sponsorship is based upon the well-known principle of Occam's razor, which holds that, *all things considered, the simplest answer is the right answer.* I remind you of this basic precept because I want to underscore the fact that there is nothing new or complex about what I discuss in this book. I simply take you back to basics, to acquaint (or reacquaint) you with the foundational elements of a successful project, so that you can apply them to your experience as a project sponsor. This book will show you how to:

- Cultivate a culture of integrity and accountability in your workplace;

- Clearly delineate between the role of the project sponsor and the project manager;

- Maximize the usefulness of project-management methodologies;

- Ask the key questions that will give you the opportunity to make fully informed decisions; and

- Think critically to gain new insight into your process as a project sponsor.

A Note on the Examples Used in This Book

The examples in this book focus on technology, because that's my area of expertise. However, the basic principles they illustrate can be applied across all industries, for any type of project.

Your organization may have unique terms for the project-management documents and procedures I discuss. For instance, what I call a "project charter" might be known as a "project proposal" or "project initiation document" in your company. Rest assured that, though the names may change, their purpose and importance stay the same. For samples and templates of the documents referenced in this book, visit my website, www.successfulprojectsponsorship.com.

Critical Thinking Questions

Each chapter ends with a set of critical thinking questions. My goal here is to jumpstart your thinking and inspire you to ask yourself the hard questions that need addressing if you're going to lead a project to a successful outcome. For example, before we begin, ask yourself:

- Am I satisfied with the level of project success in my organization, or is there room for improvement?

- Am I ready, as a project sponsor, to question my methods of leadership when it comes to projects and be willing to learn a better approach?

Chapter 1
The Role of the Project Sponsor

Sam stood in front of his white board, marker in hand, waiting for inspiration to strike. He was trying to brainstorm ways he could ensure that this project would be different from past projects. He had great project managers. He had great people. That wasn't the problem. But there seemed to be some essential ingredient missing…What was it?

"Hey, Sam, I saw your email—you wanted to speak to me?"

Sam looked up to see project manager Sarah Jones in the doorway. "Hey, Sarah. Thanks for dropping by."

"No problem. What's going on?"

"We're embarking on a new project."

Sarah raised her eyebrows, questioning. "What kind of new project?"

"A new accounts payable system—and I want this to be our most successful project yet."

"Great," Sarah said. She nodded and smiled, but Sam picked up on a hesitation in her voice. Normally Sarah was a real team player, but…this wasn't the enthusiasm he'd hoped for.

"Is something wrong?"

"Oh, it's nothing," Sarah said quickly.

"If there's a problem, you can tell me," Sam assured her. He and Sarah had always had a good rapport.

"It's just…I get the sense that people are still pretty worn out after the last project. They worked *really* hard, and, to be honest, they aren't proud of the end result."

Sam took a deep breath. As tempting as it was to paint a bright picture, Sarah was right. Her team had pushed out a quick turnaround project on a timeline that the board had demanded. He hadn't sponsored that one, but the executive who had was a real "make it happen at all costs" type of guy. And yeah, it was common knowledge that it was a bit of a dud.

"Sarah, we're turning over a new leaf. I'm serious." He uncapped his marker, ready to take some notes. "I'm fully committed to making this our best project yet."

Sarah's face lit up. "I like the sound of that," she said. "Can I help?"

"Definitely," Sam said. "I have a bird's-eye view of this company, but you have the view from the ground. There's gotta be a way that we can capitalize on that, use it to our advantage. How can we help each other?"

…

A Project Sponsor's Top Five Responsibilities

According to the Project Management Institute, "Too often, the term 'project sponsor' conjures up the image of a disconnected executive whose main responsibility is to secure the project funds and then come in for the victory lap when it is all over."[1] This disconnection stems from either an unhealthy corporate culture or just a simple misunderstanding of what the sponsor can and should bring to the process. Though the sponsor plays a crucial role in the success of a project, that role

---

1 Project Management Institute, *Executive Engagement: The Role of the Sponsor*, http://www.pmi.org/Business-Solutions/~/media/PDF/Business-Solutions/Executive%20Engagement_FINAL.ashx.

is rarely clear. In fact, in most organizations, it's quite possible that no one—neither the sponsor, the project manager, nor the project team—has any real understanding of it. As I see it, there are five top responsibilities for any great sponsor, no matter the industry or project:

1. Own the Project

David West, author of *Project Sponsorship: An Essential Guide for Those Sponsoring Projects within Their Organizations*, refers to the project sponsor as the "guardian of the investment."[2] You are responsible for the governance of the project at its highest level, which includes creating a vision for the project; getting buy-in from board members, managers, and stakeholders; and securing funding and resources.

Please do not make the mistake of thinking that this only happens at the beginning of the project. As the guardian, you must keep a watchful eye over the entire process. You are the one person in the project who has a bird's-eye view of the process and the company-wide ramifications, as well as the muscle to actually create change or get employees the support they need. From start to finish, your words and actions must demonstrate that you are personally invested and committed to the success of the project.

2. Get Your Hands Dirty

It's common for sponsors to take a hands-off approach, but the best sponsors are the ones who get their hands dirty. They are the ones who review the documents, ask probing questions, and—if the answers aren't satisfactory—follow up.

---

[2] David West, "The Elusive Project Sponsor," Wellingtone Project Management (blog), http://www.wellingtone.co.uk/news/the-elusive-project-sponsor/.

This might seem too nitty-gritty, especially if your company has a culture in which executives sponsor from afar and offer only high-level strategy. But, as the saying goes, you have to "inspect what you expect." Meaning, it's your responsibility to inspect the work you've asked your team to perform. This requires getting a close look at it, and making time in your schedule to do so. You may think that most of these day-to-day tasks are the role of the project manager, but the project manager can only act effectively with your hands-on support. The project manager will undoubtedly have great knowledge of the day-to-day challenges and successes facing the project team, but most project managers don't wield the power necessary to right the ship if it starts to stray off course. They can only recommend course corrections—you have the power to affect them. And if you're out of the loop on the micro level, you won't have the full information necessary to make great decisions at the macro level.

3. Ask Questions—and Follow Up

You'll find—especially at first, as you set new and higher standards for your employees—that when you ask critical questions, the answers will be unsatisfactory. For instance, when you review the project plan, you might ask, "Did your team agree to these task deadlines?" And the answer may very well be, "Err…no, but I know they can meet them." Though you want to be able to trust your project manager, a plan created without input from the team is a plan to fail. If your project manager presents you with such a plan, then you must say, "Well, ask the team, and bring this back to me for a second review when you've updated it based on your team's input." And then, make sure that the updated plan is delivered.

To make follow-up as painless as possible, you can ask right then and there that the person report in on a certain day.

Set a clear deadline and note it in your calendar. And when the day rolls around, make sure to check in. It won't take long before your team realizes that you are serious about following up. The more rigidly you stick to your review and follow-up processes, the sooner your team will start delivering acceptable documents on the first try.

4. Advocate for Your Project Team

One of the challenging aspects of project sponsorship is that you're beholden to many people. You must satisfy the board, management, and stakeholders—but you must also advocate for your project team. There will be times when you find yourself between the proverbial rock and hard place, as there will inevitably be clashing interests between these many groups. I strongly encourage you to listen to your project team. They are the people who actually carry out the work, which means they live within the reality of the project, and are in the best position to give a truthful assessment of its quality and progress. If you do not advocate for your project team, who will?

5. Exercise Honest Communication

You've probably experienced this at some point in your career: A manager gives a heartfelt speech about how his or her "door is always open," and encourages you to come by to talk about any concerns. But, in reality, when you do approach them with a concern, they're unavailable or dismissive. This is very common, unfortunately, and is a quick way to shut down honest communication between you and your people. No one wants to be seen as the troublemaker or squeaky wheel, but there may exist an unacknowledged culture of fear in your organization, where people have been taught that there are repercussions for speaking up—or, even worse, admitting that they've made a mistake.

It's time to go beyond encouraging honest communication; it's time to *exercise* it. This is an active process. Does it take time and energy to listen to your employees and address their problems? Indeed it does. But it's much easier to take care of a small problem than it is to wait until it escalates into a big problem. The process is as simple as you think it is: Invite your people to talk to you. When they do, listen to what they have to say. Then ask, "What can I do to help?" It may be that there is no solution—maybe he or she just needed to be heard—but if there is something you can do to ease their stress, follow up on it. What you spend in time, you'll gain a thousand-fold in the strong relationships you cultivate with your team.

Integrity: The Essential Quality That Underlies It All

Integrity is the essential foundation for all five of the responsibilities listed above. A person of integrity identifies their core values and uses those values as a measuring stick to judge any given situation. A person of integrity not only talks a good talk, but they walk it too. Their words and actions reinforce each other. You're most likely a person of integrity, or else you wouldn't be reading this book, but I encourage you to ask yourself: Are you clear on your core values? When situations get tough, do you hold to those values? Is there room for improvement?

In my experience, I've found that a project that lacks integrity in its foundation usually lacks integrity in its so-called finished product. I say "so-called" because often a hallmark of these projects is that they are not truly finished. They may have been pushed live, but they're of low quality or haven't been properly tested. They are only deemed to be finished because they met the deadline. Does this scenario seem familiar?: A project announcement says something to the effect of "The launch went great. We met our expected date, and in just two years the new system will be fully functional." It takes no time at all for people to get the real message: that, for two years, they will struggle with a subpar system. They will be frustrated and resentful for the two years it takes to fix the problems that should have been resolved prior to go-live.

It may be tempting to put up smoke and mirrors in an attempt to satisfy expectations and put the best face on the situation, but this is a short-term fix at best. Your employees will see through these tactics at once, which will cause them to lose faith in you as a manager. And when the project's flaws are inevitably revealed, as they most certainly will be, your reputation will be damaged within your company. In fact, your reputation will suffer doubly, since it will be perceived that you delivered a subpar project *and* tried to pull the wool over the collective eyes.

I don't mean to sound grim or to suggest that you're lacking in personal integrity. But what I do want to underscore is that, while it might seem like an intangible quality, integrity is absolutely crucial to the health of your projects, your team, and your personal reputation. I encourage you to define integrity for yourself and then model it to your employees, colleagues, and managers. If there is a lack of integrity in your organization, it may come as a shock to people when you begin to implement higher standards. A good analogy is the "broken windows" theory, which holds that a neighborhood attracts more unsavory behavior when windows are broken and buildings are covered in graffiti. If there's been a lack of integrity in your organization, people might resist your efforts to clean it up. But stay strong. If you show them that the "windows" in your department can't be broken, you'll establish yourself as a person of integrity, and people will come to respect it and expect it from you.

Critical Thinking Questions

- How do I define integrity? (Consider making a list of the essential qualities that make up your personal sense of integrity. That way, you'll always have a measuring stick by which to judge a situation.)

- Do I encourage open, honest assessment of the project and its progress?

- Do I reward integrity in my people, or do I dismiss or gloss over employees' concerns or behaviors?

Chapter 2
Communicating the Project Purpose

Sam had a spring in his step as he made his way to his meeting with project manager Sarah and Benjamin Black, the director of accounts payable. He and Sarah had a great meeting the week before, and he was feeling genuinely optimistic about the future. It wasn't going to be easy. He'd traditionally fashioned himself as more of a "hands-off" type of sponsor, not one to meddle in the daily goings-on of a project. But Sarah had really turned him around on that one. He hadn't realized some of the challenges she'd faced in the past—especially when it came to coordinating across departments. It made him see that he could better empower her work, and it wouldn't take too much time from his own schedule.

Sam, Sarah, and Benjamin settled around the conference table, coffee cups in hand, to discuss the vision for the process. Right away, Benjamin spoke up. "I know the board is going to want this live within six months," he said. "So I hope your team is ready to hustle."

Sam groaned inwardly when he saw a small frown pass across Sarah's face. She looked toward him pointedly. Guess this was his first trial. "Well, Benjamin, I think we need to back up a bit…maybe get a sense of the scope before we start throwing out deadlines. What do you think, Sarah?"

Sarah looked encouraged. "I agree. With all due respect, there's just no way to estimate how long the project will take if we don't know how much work it will entail."

Benjamin laughed. "Well, good thing Sam's the sponsor on this one—he can tell that to the guys upstairs."

That was a somewhat grim prospect to Sam. But that had been one of Sarah's top requests when he'd asked "How can I help?" She said the best sponsors she'd ever had were advocates for the team, especially when it came to negotiating reasonable deadlines. "How about this," Sam suggested. "We outline our ideal vision for the project, and Sarah can work with the team to estimate how long it will take. And when the estimated timeline is determined, if the board insists on a shorter deadline, we can look into scaling down the scope or modifying the timeline to one that is mutually agreed upon."

"Sounds way too logical," Benjamin cracked. "That's not the way we do it around here."

"Benjamin, I think you're going to be pleasantly surprised," Sam said. "You'll just have to wait and see. Now, about that scope…"

...

It's no coincidence that, in trying to create better habits within his organization, Sam brought together Sarah and Benjamin to have a conversation before creating the project charter. These three are crucial players, who each bring a different—and important—perspective to the project: Sam as the guardian and owner of the effort; Sarah as the point person for the employees responsible for executing the tasks; and Benjamin as the manager of the group that will eventually live with the completed project.

At the start of any project, it's important to have an initial sit-down, as Sam did, so that the sponsor, project manager, and any other involved executives can get on the same page. Each has a separate, but connected, stake in the effort, and their presence at this initial meeting ensures that all angles will be accounted for. The project manager will use this as his or her starting point for gathering the necessary information for the project charter, so it's imperative that this meeting happens and that all parties share the same commitment to quality and integrity. The result will be a project charter that accurately captures the vision and priorities of the project and the people involved. And a great charter is the first step toward a great finish.

What to Look for in a Project Charter

The project charter is a high-level document that articulates the vision and rationale for the project, and lays the foundation from which all other efforts will spring. It's important to ensure that this step is not skipped or glossed over, and that you give it a thorough review to catch any missing pieces or problems. Ideally, this concise (five to seven pages) document should be created by your project manager with input from you and the team, and should include the following elements:

- **Statement of purpose.** The project charter should clearly articulate the purpose and desired outcomes of the project, in a way that can be readily understood by the team who will be completing the work. This answers the crucial question of "why." If your team doesn't understand why the company is undertaking the project, and what the expected outcome and benefits will be, there's no way they will be able to buy in with any real enthusiasm. Realize that the team may have ideas about what needs to be delivered to meet your "why." If you are clear on the desired result, let their expertise be valued in determining the "how." You may be pleasantly surprised by the innovative solutions that present themselves.

- **A list of the parties involved.** This should include the team members all the way up to those responsible for the governance of the project. This list lets people know who to go to for approvals or escalations.

- **Scope.** The project charter should be crystal clear in conveying what is in scope for the project and what is out of scope. It's important to fully think through the scope, as it will draw a much-needed boundary around the project and prevent "scope creep"; i.e., the gradual expansion of the scope (and time and cost…) beyond what was initially conveyed in the charter.

- **Deliverables.** Clearly articulate the desired deliverables so that each team member knows the expected outcome of the project. Only when they know the expected outcome will they be able to envision their particular role in achieving it.

- **Critical success items.** In addition to laying the foundation at the beginning of a project, the charter should serve as a review document at the end, so that you and the project team can determine whether the critical deliverables and values were met. For example, if one of the goals of the accounts payable system is to pay 50 percent more invoices with any available discounts taken, then the charter must state this goal, along with measuring the level of discounts that were taken prior to the start of the project.

The Date

When envisioning a new project, it's not uncommon for an organization's leadership to decide on a particular deadline. Of course, sometimes the deadline is mandated by outside forces, such as the enactment of new legislation. Usually, though, the date comes about like this: "We'd like to have a new accounts payable system up and running before our busy season in June." And so, a date is decided. The desire may very well be predicated on a legitimate business need, but the problem is that the date is rarely decided with input from those employees who will actually perform the work. Meaning, the date is likely not based on real information. Whatever the reasons, though, the date is decided from above and is then solidified and incentivized, either by the promise of a reward or the threat of a punishment. With powerful incentives in place, The Date becomes the project's driving force.

Of course, the best way to get a realistic date is to ask your team. If you've outlined clear deliverables, and the team has had an opportunity to estimate the time needed, this will spell success for all. However, as reasonable as this is, as project sponsor, you may find yourself having to push back against deadlines that will endanger the quality of the end result or put an undue burden of stress on the project team. Please *do* push back. It will be worth it in the end. And, if the date is truly nonnegotiable, I encourage you to push back and advocate for your people in other ways, such as trimming the scope or negotiating to get the team extra resources. With a little creative thinking, there is almost always a solution that will satisfy all parties.

The Official Kickoff

Once the project charter is finalized, then comes the kickoff meeting. This meeting is attended by the project sponsor and any other involved executives, the project manager, and the entire project team. This is your opportunity to meet face-to-face (or at least by conference call) with everyone who will be affected by the project and who will contribute to its eventual success. This isn't a job that can be delegated; please find a way to fit this kickoff meeting into your schedule. If you don't, the message you send to your team is that this project isn't a high priority. This is your opportunity to get everyone on board; to get them to buy in to the project on both a professional and personal level. This is your chance to get them excited! Yes, this is a business meeting, but don't be afraid to motivate your team and rally their enthusiasm. They want the company to thrive, and if you can communicate how the scope and purpose of this particular project will help the company thrive—and that they, the team, are crucial to that success—chances are, they'll be on board.

Critical Thinking Questions

- How clear is my team on the purpose of what I have asked them to do? Can they articulate that purpose back to me?

- Did the team have input in defining the work needed to achieve the goal? Are their concerns and ideas reflected in the project charter?

- Have I ensured that clear timelines have been established, and that there's a reasonable chance that they can be met?

- Did I attend the kickoff meeting and use it as an opportunity to inspire my team?

Chapter 3
Getting Specific with a Real Project Plan

Sam walked away from the kickoff meeting feeling great. For the first time in a long time, the project charter balanced the desires of the business with the needs of the people, and he sensed a tentative excitement in the team. The project would be a challenge, for sure, but definitely doable, given that the scope and timeline were in step with each other. He'd been able to persuade the board to approve a nine-month timetable rather than the six-month timetable they'd initially asked for. It had been somewhat awkward—the board was in the habit of having it their way—but he'd gone in prepared to make his case and justify the need for more time, and it had worked. Looking around at the smiling faces at the kickoff meeting, he was very glad of it.

Sam turned around to see Sarah, the project manager, walking behind him. "That went well," he said.

"It did," Sarah agreed. "I think they actually have hope for this project."

"I do hear that hope springs eternal…" Sam quipped. "So, I suppose I'll just sit back and wait for the first status report to roll in, right?"

"Well…" Sarah hesitated.

"What is it?"

"Since we're turning over a new leaf and all, would you be willing to look over the project plan?"

Sam was confused. "Isn't that what we just did?"

"That was the project *charter*. Next up is the project plan—that's where we break out the project into tasks."

Sam had never reviewed a project plan before. He thought of his overstuffed calendar and was tempted to delegate or explain that this was too detailed for him. Did he even have time for this? What insight would he be able to offer? But like she said—a new leaf. He didn't want to shut down their lines of communication when they'd just barely gotten open. "Okay," he said, a bit reluctantly.

...

If you, like our friend Sam, have never laid eyes on a project plan, you're not alone. Typically, this part of the process has been deemed too "in the weeds" for most project sponsors, since most have been taught to lead from afar. Please do not make the mistake of thinking that the project plan is out of your purview. It takes only a modest amount of time and brainpower to do a great assessment of a project plan, and there's no telling how much stress and hassle you'll save yourself and your team by catching potential problems at the start and nipping them in the bud. In this chapter, I'll outline the basics of a project plan and point out the elements that you should be paying close attention to.

What to Look for in a Project Plan

Whereas the charter painted a picture of the project in broad brush strokes, outlining the scope and goals, the project plan is where the nitty-gritty details get sorted out. It includes a timetable for the project, assigns the person who is working on each task, and includes a cascade of dependencies showing how all of the tasks are interrelated.

The project plan is a critical foundational document that will steer the entire project, and it's crucial that you sit down with your project manager, and any other interested parties, to do an early review. Though I don't recommend that you consult the project plan daily, weekly, or even monthly, it is crucial to have at least one meeting to review it. This way, you can confirm that a project plan exists (yes, this is extremely basic, but you would be amazed by how often this step is overlooked) and that it reflects the scope and purpose outlined in the project charter, as well as being done well and with input from the team.

When reviewing the project plan, ensure that it includes these critical elements. They may be called by different names in different companies, but their purpose (and importance) is the same:

- **A thorough but concise breakdown of the tasks and deadlines.** The project plan should include the major tasks and milestones of the project, but be wary of any project plan that is thousands of lines long. At this length, it is so bulky as to be totally useless to the team.

- **A sequence of events.** It doesn't matter whether the sequence is "agile," "waterfall," or any other project methodology; the bottom line is that one thing has to finish before another starts. This is called dependency.

- **A clear critical path.** This is the path of work that, when set up correctly, will tell you whether you're on track and set to meet your dates and costs.

- **Key, defined milestones for completion.** A milestone is a major deliverable. It may be called by a different name in your organization, but no matter the terminology, these key deliverables should be defined within the project plan and tied directly to the tasks. Beware of any project plan that has milestones that are linked to nothing.

If the project plan is missing any of these items, it needs to be revised. Period. These four elements are absolutely critical to a quality project, and a project cannot be expected to go forward successfully without them. As you review the plan, keep your eyes open for any red flags—such as dates that are hard-coded; meaning, the project manager set the due date, but it's not connected to any other dependencies. Don't hesitate to ask questions. Even the most seasoned project manager can miss something or introduce an error into a project plan, and you do him or her a service by pointing it out.

If the project plan does indeed include all of these critical elements, it means you're off to a good start, but you're not out of the woods yet. At this point, you can start asking deeper questions. Your first question should always be: "Who put this project plan together? Was there input from the team?" If the project manager says, "I put this together" or "I talked to the resource managers," your response should be: "Go back. Get input from the team." You must require—not simply recommend—that your project manager go to the team, or else they might not do it. And this can happen for many reasons. Your project manager is probably not being sneaky or lazy by putting together a project plan without team input. Rather, they might presume that it would take too much time to consult every member of the team. They might presume that they (the project manager) or the team members' managers will simply set the deadlines and the project team will hustle to make it work. Or they might be operating from a place of wishful thinking, and the resulting project plan is based on optimism rather than realism. Maybe "this is the way it's always been done."

Whatever the reason, your response has to be: "Go back. Get input from the team." The people doing the work are the only people who can give an accurate accounting of what all is involved in completing a task and how long it will take. They know their workload and they know their schedule. Most importantly, they know the level of time and effort that is required to complete the tasks you have asked them to do. If they're given the opportunity to review the project plan and provide feedback, then you'll know that the project plan is solid. Anything less, and you're setting the team up to fail.

Once you've confirmed that the project plan was compiled with input from the team, you can ask: "How can I help?" Ask this question sincerely—not as you're walking out the door to your next meeting. Depending on the culture at your company, the project manager might see this question as polite but empty gesture. Don't be offended. Instead, I encourage you to see this as an opportunity to turn over a new leaf in your workplace. If you consistently offer sincere help, and follow up with solutions or support, people will come around.

The Importance of Project-Planning Software

Your review of the project plan will go much more smoothly if both you and your project manager have a working knowledge of project-planning software (such as Microsoft Project), and that you actually use it. Too frequently, an organization will use a spreadsheet in lieu of proper project-planning software, and I encourage you not to make this mistake. A product like Microsoft Project is specifically designed to handle the dependencies inherent in a project. Spreadsheets are not. Without getting too granular here, a major benefit of a project-management software is that, when a task or date is changed, the program automatically updates the other line items that will be subsequently affected. Spreadsheets don't have this capability, and either your project manager will waste time re-coding the dates and tasks as changes come up, or—and this is the more likely scenario—the pseudo project plan will simply become obsolete, meaningless, and never updated.

Thinking Ahead to Testing

Testing is a crucial component of preparing a project for a successful launch, so when you review the project plan, ensure that testing hasn't been overlooked. Testers should have input into the project plan, which should include the time, budget, and resources needed for conducting tests *and* fixing defects. A good rule of thumb is to figure that 30 percent of the project timeline will be dedicated to testing and fixing defects. So, if it's a nine-month project, expect to spend three months on testing.

Tips for Effective Testing

- Require a testing strategy, with pre-defined test cases and scripts, and a point person or testing manager who is accountable for making sure this happens. Follow up to confirm the existence of a testing strategy.

- For software projects, require separate environments for developers and testers. It's all too common for there to exist only one environment, meaning that testers are attempting to test a program that can, at any moment, be changed by a developer. Talk about a moving target!

- Know that it's not enough to simply *do* the testing. The purpose of testing is to uncover issues that need to be resolved—and then resolving them.

- Make sure that testing updates are part of your status report, so you can keep abreast of issues.

- Don't force your end users to be your first testers. User acceptance testing should be a final confirmation, not the first round of testing. First time (or unit testing) is not their job. By the time you've launched your product to your users, it should have been tested and defects should have been resolved. To see how real users will interact with your product, gather focus groups.

When Defects Are Inevitably Revealed…

As project sponsor, when it comes to testing, you must advocate for the user as much as possible while also balancing the needs of the business. When bugs and defects are inevitably revealed, it's up to you to make an informed decision. Is it a bug that the company can live with? Or is it worth the time and money to fix? You can work with whomever will eventually own the product or system—in Sam Smith's case, that would be Benjamin, the director of accounts payable—to discuss the severity of the defects and decide whether they're minor enough to live with, or major enough that it perhaps merits delaying the launch so that the defects can be fixed.

Of course, it can be frustrating when months are spent developing a product or system, and then the testing results reveal major problems. It may be tempting to water down the results to downplay the potential consequences of these defects. You may be tempted to ask employees to just "live with it," or presume that they'll figure out a way to work around it. If you find yourself—or your colleagues—employing these pressure tactics, I encourage you to ask yourself why. If the answer is that you want to meet the go-live date, no matter the cost, I encourage you to rethink the situation.

There's honestly no point in testing if you're going to ignore the results, and there's no point in rolling out a new process or product if it's riddled with defects.

...

Sam was pleasantly surprised by how little time it took to give the project plan a thorough read. Why hadn't he started doing this years ago? From what he could see, the list of tasks looked comprehensive, and each had a due date and an owner. But wait…he knew for a fact that the lead developer was going on a trip to Hawaii next month—they'd just talked about it that morning in the elevator. So why was she scheduled to hit a major milestone during that timeframe? Sam puzzled through that, wondering if it were a mistake. Well, why not ask the project manager? He picked up the phone on his desk and rang her extension.

"Sarah, I have a question for you about this project plan."

"Sure, Sam."

"How do you go about assigning the deadlines for individual tasks?"

"I create a schedule and then distributed it to the team," Sarah said. "Why do you ask?"

"Well, I see that your lead developer is slated to hit a milestone during the time she'll be on vacation in Hawaii."

Sarah groaned. "Ugh, I forgot all about her vacation."

"So, wouldn't it make more sense to have folks tell *you* what kind of timeframe they need for completing their assignments, rather than the other way around?"

"Well…this is just the way we've always done it, Sam."

Sarah sounded a bit defensive, and for a moment Sam wondered whether he should back off. He didn't want Sarah to think he was micromanaging—nor did he have time to micromanage, frankly. That's why they hired project managers in the first place. "How about this?" he said. "We try a new tactic for this project, and if it doesn't work, we can always go back to our old ways."

Sarah was silent for a moment. Finally, she said, "Okay, I'll give it a whirl. It's going to take longer this way, though."

"Well, if I hadn't done this review, you would be working from a flawed project plan—since I'm sure your lead developer isn't going to want to code while sitting on a beach. So aren't I saving you from wasting time in the future?"

"That's true. Putting in the extra time now will save us from unpleasant surprises down the road."

"Okay, get the new deadlines and have them to me in an hour."

"Sam!" Sarah was indignant. "I can't possibly—"

"—I'm just kidding, Sarah," Sam said, smiling. "You tell me: When do *you* think you'll be able to follow up with your team and finalize the project plan?"

"Very funny, Sam," Sarah said dryly.

"Thank you, thank you. I'll be here all week."

"Okay, well, I can have the new project plan on your desk by Friday."

"Great."

...

The Importance of Accountability

People do their best work when they've got "skin in the game." If you keep people accountable for the failure or success of their endeavors, everyone benefits. I encourage you to create a culture wherein, if an employee makes a promise to get work done, they do it, whether that means working overtime, adding more people to their team—whatever it takes. But it's important to keep in mind that accountability only works if all parties have agreed to the terms. This is why team input is such a crucial component of a successful project plan. If each team member has a chance to set realistic expectations for their tasks—and if their voices are heard and reflected in the project plan—they'll have an automatic buy-in to their own accountability, because they set the task deadline themselves. It didn't come from above. It came from within. It's easier to hold someone accountable for a rule they set themselves.

Some project managers and team members will be resistant to the idea of owning specific tasks, putting them in writing, and being accountable for them. You might find this surprising, since project charters, plans, and accountability all increase the likelihood for success. But employees may be hesitant to take responsibility for their part of the project, because they may see themselves as taking on a personal risk. There's fear there. This is understandable, since so many projects fail and so many companies have a culture of silence, where employees are met with negative consequences if they speak up. If I "own" a risk, it means I'm responsible for raising hard questions and being the "squeaky wheel" if necessary. If questioners have been deemed troublemakers in your company, it's understandable that folks will need some real encouragement to speak up. But rest assured, if you instill these principles, it'll only take one or two run-throughs before your employees are on board. If people are held accountable for the tasks and risks, do them a favor in return and hold them accountable for their successes too. (You'll read more about this in chapter 8, "Recognizing Your Team.")

Critical Thinking Questions

- Did I give the project plan at least one thorough review?

- Did I check to make sure that all components of the plan, including testing, have been accounted for? Did

I watch for "gotchas" such as hard-coded dates and milestones?

- Am I clear on what critical dependencies are and how I can influence and support those milestones in getting done on time while maintaining their quality?

- Did I follow up with my project manager to resolve any questions or concerns that came up during my review of the project plan?

Chapter 4
Managing Risk

By its very nature, a project is a future-focused endeavor, and therefore risky. You're out on a limb, trying something that your company hasn't tried before. Of course you shore up against risk by hiring a skilled team, conducting market research, thinking through the possible outcomes, and so forth—but risks are inherent in the process, and mistakes will be made. By you. By your project manager. By your project team. Get comfortable with this fact as soon as possible and you'll spare yourself a lot of agony. Risks are what make a project challenging. Challenges are what make a project rewarding. And mistakes are simply a necessary byproduct of the process. You have to break some eggs, as they say. In this chapter, I discuss how to uncover the risks and deal with them.

...

Sam was at his desk. He looked up at the sound of a knock at the door and saw Sarah smiling in at him. "Did you get my risk list?" she asked.

"I did," Sam said wryly. In fact, he was holding it right that very moment, wiping off the coffee that he'd spat all over it. "In fact, I've added something to it myself."

"You did?" Sarah's eyebrows lifted in surprise.

"Yes—my coffee. I choked on it when I saw the number of risks on this list!"

"Well, I did try something different."

"There are thirty-two risks on this list, Sarah! Usually there are only four or five. Are you trying to tell me this project is doomed?"

"Nope, not at all," Sarah said confidently. "This project is no more risky than any other project—it's just that this list is more comprehensive."

"What good does that do, besides setting me up for a heart attack?"

Sarah gestured at one of the chairs across from Sam's desk. "Do you have a minute to hear about it?"

"Sure, sure."

"Well, I ran a risk workshop. It was actually a lot of fun, if you can believe it. Let me tell you about it…"

...

Why a Risk List?

The risk list is a centralized holding pen for all of the anxieties that keep your team up at night. The quality and severity of these risks can vary widely, and they can be of a professional or personal nature. "This vendor has been unreliable lately, and I'm afraid they won't deliver on time." "Our cutover plan for the last project was terrible, and I'm afraid that will happen again." "I'm afraid I won't be able to get my work done before I leave for my trip to go backpacking through Malaysia."

The benefit of creating such a list is so that (a) every team member can know their concerns have been accounted for; (b) every risk can be assigned to an owner, who will be responsible for doing their very best to ensure that the risk doesn't come to fruition; and (c) so that you as the sponsor can have full knowledge of all risks associated with the project.

It's typical to see lists with only four or five risks. This is almost always a bad sign, as it usually means that the risk list was generated by the project manager, without input from the team. A short list is not a sign that there are only a few risks. A short list is a sign that the project manager didn't mine thoroughly enough. This is dangerous, because it creates a false sense of security—and most certainly sets you up for some nasty surprises down the road. Just because a risk doesn't make it to the list, it doesn't mean it can't create trouble. Though you may be initially shocked—as our friend Sam was—at the number of line items on a very thorough risk list, rest assured that twenty to forty risks is normal. And when they've all been accounted for, you and your team will feel confident in the fact that you'll be making decisions based on complete knowledge. Forewarned is forearmed, as they say.

The Risk Workshop

The risk workshop is the forum in which the risk list is generated. This is an in-person roundtable, led by the project manager, with the entire team in attendance. Your presence isn't necessary—and in fact, depending on the culture at your organization, might cause people to feel too inhibited to air their concerns (though that might turn around when you've proven your commitment to honest communication). However, it's important that, as a sponsor, you know what goes into a good risk workshop. This will enable you to identify whether your team is doing well or needs to make some improvements.

To kick off the risk workshop, the project manager asks, "What about this project keeps you up at night?"

From there, each member of the team takes a turn presenting one perceived risk—only one. Generally, people have multiple causes for concern, but I find that the conversation is most effective by turn-taking. Team members should state their risks as an "if, then" proposition. For example, "If the system isn't tested well, then it could have defects going live." Or, "If the systems aren't properly integrated, then I won't be able to run the report I need."

For each risk presented, the project manager should help the team member identify the risk index. Those risks with the highest risk index are given special focus, so it's important that this number is generated. To identify the risk index, the project manager should ask two questions:

- **"On a scale of 1 to 5, how likely is it to happen?"** (1 being "very unlikely" and 5 being "almost definitely")

- **"On a scale of 1 to 5, if it does happen, how great will its impact be?"** (1 being "it won't make much of a difference at all" and 5 being "the project will fail completely")

You can then do some simple math to identify the risk index: multiply the first number by the second number. The lowest possible risk index is 1 (1x1), while the highest is 25 (5x5). With this information, you can identify the risks with the highest risk factor so that you can give them the greatest amount of attention.

After the risk and its index have both been identified, the project manager should move on to the next person. The risk workshop needs to move at a steady clip so that everyone has a chance to sufficiently air their concerns. The conversation should move from one person to the next until everyone runs out of risks. Oftentimes during the process, one person's risk will remind another person of a risk they hadn't thought of; that's why it's so important to have this workshop in person, so you can take advantage of the "water cooler effect." People encourage each other; they laugh and tell stories—it can be a surprisingly fun process. And, at the end of the workshop, the project manager should have a list of twenty to forty risks.

It should be noted that the point of the workshop is merely to generate the list—not to problem solve, as it's not an efficient use of time to do so.

The final step of the workshop is to assign each risk an owner. After the workshop, the project manager should visit each team member individually to say, "You own such-and-such risk. How are you going to prevent it from happening?" This gives each owner an opportunity to come up with a strategy for mitigating the risk. Now, that doesn't mean the risk will never blossom into an "issue"; and sometimes the fix is too expensive or time-consuming, and can't be done. Usually, though, there is a solution, and the project manager and the risk owner—with support from the project sponsor, if necessary—can come up with a plan for either avoiding the risk altogether or minimizing its impact if it does become an issue. And the overall benefit to you is that you can be confident that, when a risk does become an issue, you'll be making an informed decision.

What's the Sponsor's Role in Dealing with the Risk List?

- Require that the project manager run a risk workshop and generate a risk list with full participation of the team.

- Though your attendance at the risk workshop isn't required, consider participating—but only if you've established an honest rapport with your team and feel confident that they won't be shy about airing their concerns in front of you.

- When you receive the risk list, ask "How can I help?"

- Identify the risks with the highest risk factor, and be sure that the risk owner has brainstormed contingency plans. You may have to help or provide encouragement to be sure the owner feels empowered enough to provide a plan.

- Make sure that the mitigation plans get translated into action items on the project plan.

...

Despite his initial dismay, Sam was impressed by Sarah's handling of the risk list. From what he could tell, she'd encouraged a really honest conversation with her team, and had dug deep, thinking of all the possible pitfalls. It was strangely reassuring, Sam thought, to know that no stone had been left unturned. He thought he'd probably sleep better at night knowing that Sarah had identified as many of the risks as possible and created contingency plans for what would be done if—or when—the risks morphed into issues.

"Sarah, what can I do to help mitigate these risks?"

"I'm glad you asked." Sarah picked up the list and pointed to one of the line items. "What keeps *me* up at night is *this*—worrying about systems integration. If the new accounts payable system isn't properly integrated with the system they use in purchasing, we'll have a real mess on our hands. None of the vendor information they input will make it into the accounts payable database."

"Is purchasing not cooperating?"

"I have no idea. No one over there has time to meet with me."

"Hmm," Sam said. "That's a problem. I'll contact the manager over there and see if I can catch their attention. I'll get them to assign someone who can be a point of contact for you. It's obviously crucial that they're supportive of this effort."

Sarah's eyes lit up. "Thanks, Sam. That would be great. I'll be able to rest a little easier once that happens."

...

When Risks Become Issues...

Inevitably, some risks will become a reality, at which point they're referred to as "issues." The question isn't whether things will go wrong, but when and how badly. I encourage you to make it your business to know about issues as soon as they arise. Presuming you followed my advice from back in chapter 1 and fostered an environment of open communication, this won't be a problem. If you reward your people for integrity, and for being bold enough to identify an issue as soon it shows its face, they will come to you early and often, which will make issues much less painful to resolve.

It takes courage to identify a problem and escalate it. Issues are just as frustrating for your people as they are for you, and, too often, sponsors compound their employees' pain by dismissing their concerns—or worse, placing blame. That's why it's so important that sponsors show integrity even in the face of problems or failure. These moments are proving grounds; they will show your employees whether you meant what you said when you promised to support them. If you do not offer enthusiastic guidance and support when it's needed most, your employees will presume that your earlier promises were just empty gestures.

Also, don't let issues get lost in translation. If your project manager comes to you, waving red flags, you may be tempted to perform some verbal magic when reporting up the chain. Suddenly a red flag becomes "We're green…with just a couple problems, but they're being handled." This short-term balm is just that—*short term*. I encourage you to instead play a long game. See problems as an opportunity to be a great leader. If you're made aware of a problem and you embrace the opportunity to fix it, you strengthen not only the project itself but also your relationships with your team.

Critical Thinking Questions

- Have I allowed myself to be fully aware of the project's risks? Can I state the top five risks that could sink the project if they become issues?

- Have I made sure there is a mitigation plan for the identified risks, or have I cultivated an attitude of "I'll cross that bridge when I come to it"?

- Have I made sure that the manager in charge of this effort has followed up and verified that the risks have been addressed long before they become issues?

- Do I jump on issues as soon as they arise and follow through on my promises of support?

- Have I fostered an environment in which the project manager and team are willing to speak up when things go off-course?

Chapter 5
Project Status and Communication During Execution

It was a couple weeks into the project and Sam was anxious to see a status report. Sarah had promised him the first one that day. He decided to turn the tables for a change and drop by her office. "Knock knock," he said.

Sarah looked up from her computer. "Hey, Sam, how's it going?"

"That's what I'm here to find out," he said. "How's the project coming along?"

"So far, so good. I'm working up a status report right now. Want to see?" Sarah turned her monitor and beckoned Sam to sit down. "I'm trying to make these reports more useful to you, so it would be great to have your input."

"Okay." Sam glanced at the report on her screen. "Looks good to me," he said with a shrug. "I see a pie chart…and a green stoplight. What more could I want? Looks like the project is on track."

Sarah sat back and crossed her arms. "Do you have any idea what a green light means, Sam?"

"Is this a trick question? I presume it means the project is running on time and on budget."

Sarah sighed. "I wish you were right. But…to be honest, most sponsors in this company get…well, they freak out when a project goes to yellow or red. They don't want to see yellow until the project is *months* overdue."

"Months?!" Sam's jaw dropped. "Well…that explains a lot."

"Like how projects are continually in the green—until the day a project manager comes to you to admit that the project is over budget and overdue?" Sarah looked nervous for a moment. "I don't want to get anyone in trouble," she said quickly. "But I figure, since we've committed to honest communication, I should come clean. We do the best we can to keep projects on target, but…I've known project managers who were taken off the project because the status went red."

"Sounds like a classic case of shooting the messenger," Sam said. He was embarrassed to hear that something like that had happened in his company. "Well, I'd rather you tell it like it is, if you don't mind."

"Good!" Sarah clapped her hands. "What I'd like to do is find out exactly what kind of information *you* want to see on a weekly basis, and how *you* want to define green, yellow, and red…"

…

Now, I don't want to insult our friend Sam, but he's not too savvy in the way of status reports. Like all sponsors, he wants to be kept in the loop with regular updates. But he hasn't invested much energy into figuring out whether the information he's getting is of high quality. He takes a quick scan to see a familiar-looking pie chart and the green-yellow-red "stoplight" graphic, but he should be digging more deeply than that. In my experience, I've seen too many status reports that were a feat of PowerPoint artistry—slide after slide crammed with colors, shapes, and charts, and line upon line of data presented in six-point font. They look great, but are oftentimes meaningless.

How does this happen? I assure you, it's not that your project team is a bunch of con artists. Usually, if status reports are being whitewashed to reflect the team's perception of what the sponsor "wants" to see, it's a symptom that a culture of fear is pervading your organization. We'll talk more about this later in the chapter.

Luckily, Sam and Sarah have both committed to transparent communication. This means they can work together to co-create a status system that gets them on the same page and provides Sam with the honest information he needs to make well-informed decisions. Let's look at what a great status report should look like.

The Essentials of Status Reporting

First off, frequency. How often you review a status report will depend on the timeline of the project, but a good rule of thumb is to request a report on a weekly basis. This ensures that you'll be made aware of issues as soon as they arise, so you can deal with them before they drag the project off course.

Second, content. Your status report can be customized in any way you like, so if there is a particular piece of data you'd like to see, you can request it of your project manager. The report should be made available to everyone, as a way of fostering open communication and complete transparency among the team. (And if you do need confidential information, ask for it to be put into a separate status report.) In general, a thorough status report should address the following questions:

- What did the team accomplish this week? This should be five bullets or less.

- What will they accomplish next week? This should be five bullets or less.

- What are the top risks? These are the top items from the risk list that are still active and could still cause the project to fail in some way.

- What are the current issues? As mentioned earlier, issues are risks that have come to pass and need to be addressed.

- What are the top critical path milestones, and what percentage of each is complete?

- What is the overall status? This is an informed rating, based on the other items combined.

A popular component of a status report is the ubiquitous "green, yellow, red" designation. Here, in a general sense, is what those colors *should* mean: Green means "We're on track and things are progressing as they should be." Yellow means "There's cause for concern. We are in danger of missing our date." Red means "We missed it! The date has passed." Now, these colors can be defined any way you want—you're the sponsor. What's important, though, is that if your company uses this system, they use it in a truthful manner. In some organizations, it's not uncommon for a project to stay at a green status until the project is *many months off track*. Only then will they push the status to yellow. This is obviously not an accurate representation of the project's progress.

Most sponsors hate to see red, and project managers are reluctant to include a red light in their status report. But believe it or not, red is a good thing; it means you're getting honest information from your project manager. It's better to know that there's a problem, because that's the only way you can deal with it. If your project manager is afraid to show red, it means that there's a fear-inducing message or attitude coming down from you, the project sponsor, as well as other executives or the company culture in general. If project managers aren't empowered to be truthful in their status reports, then a status report becomes a meaningless document and a waste of time. Don't hobble this crucial mode of communication by using it as a tool for delusion rather than truth.

And remember: status reporting doesn't need to be a one-way street. It's not all about the project manager sending information to you—you can feel free to check in. Don't be shy! Pop in, get to know people. You can support them even by just listening. How easy is that?

Questioning and Following Up on a Status Report

When reviewing a status report, stay attuned to anything that appears to have been whitewashed, and trust your gut if it seems like something is wrong. Be sure to question anything that looks to be a red flag or simply requires some follow-up. For instance, if the status report indicates that a milestone has been missed, ask your project manager: "Since this milestone wasn't met, was a new date set? How will this change affect the next items downstream? Has missing this milestone introduced any new risks to the project?"

I've said it before and I'll say it again: Follow-up is crucial. Keep asking questions, and let your people know that you're there—in part to keep them accountable to their deadlines (which they should be able to meet since they set them themselves) and in part to ask them how you can be supportive. It could be that the team is experiencing a sticking point that you, as an executive, have the power to unglue. Of course, you don't want to micromanage, nor do you have time to micromanage, but it's quite possible that you have the influence and insight to help problematic situations run more smoothly.

Bonus Tip: "Next Two Weeks" Email

I have one other communication practice that is unique to me, but that everyone loves. I'll share it with you. Awhile back I had a lead programmer tell me that he missed his deliverable dates because he didn't know what they were. It didn't matter that I had meetings with the team and provided project deadlines and so forth. He swore he was late because he didn't know the go-live date, not because he didn't do the work. It was not true, but his management defended him nonetheless.

For that reason, I created a weekly email called "Next Two Weeks." This is an email that goes to everyone on the project, from top to bottom. It's short and to the point, with information presented in easy-to-scan bullet points, and I'm completely honest about any concerns or worries that need to be expressed. This email takes just a couple minutes to read, and it always states the go-live date of the project. This way, I know for sure that no one can ever say, "But…I didn't know what our target date was!"

If you'd like to see an email like this, I'm sure your project manager would be happy to oblige. It's an easily digestible method for getting a heads-up about the mood and health of the team and the project.

...

Sam was less than pleased to open the most recent report and see that the status had been pushed to yellow. The project had been going smoothly up until now; he felt disheartened to see that it was in danger of going off track.

He sighed and leaned in to take a closer look at the report. "Just what's the problem?" He asked himself.

Testing, he saw. Apparently, the testing group hadn't finalized their strategy, as their testing lead had taken an unexpected sick leave and had been out of the office for two weeks.

The phone rang. It was Sarah. She sounded frustrated. "Things have been going so well up until now," she lamented.

"Well, don't worry—I'm sure we can get things back on track. Can't we get someone else to create the testing strategy?" Sam asked.

"I asked around, but nobody stepped up to do it. They seem kind of frazzled over there; they're short-handed and really busy right now."

"That's understandable," Sam said. "But…this accounts payable system is a priority in the company right now. I'll give a call to their manager and see if they can't make some adjustments to get this done."

"That would be *great*," Sarah said.

"Who's their manager over there…?" Sam asked, picking up the phone.

Ten minutes later, Sam hung up the phone and clapped his hands. "Crisis averted," he said triumphantly. He'd expected to have to fight to get what he wanted, but all it had taken was a little persuasion. Sarah was right—they were short-handed and running around with their hair on fire. But, after a little digging, it turned out that they were prioritizing a different project—one that was set to go live *three* months after the accounts payable system. It hadn't taken much to persuade their manager to take a pause and reassign an employee to take over where the lead tester had left off.

It looked like the testing plan would be created on time, after all.

...

Critical Thinking Questions

- What is my proven level of trust from those providing me status reports? Have they given me great information in the past, meaning I have no need to question their reports? Or have there been issues in the past, which means that a level of trust must be earned on this project?

- Is the status report intentionally busy or cluttered, so that no one will actually take the time to read it? Or does it supply all parties with critical information?

- Does the status report call out dangerous risks and new issues early so they can be addressed quickly?

- Have I engendered and encouraged a level of trust from my team so that they know I will listen to their concerns and not hide or whitewash information?

- Do I respond swiftly and appropriately when my team informs me that a "green" has turned into a "yellow"?

Chapter 6
Achieving Operational Readiness

Change can bring up a lot of questions and fears for people, and the purpose of operational readiness is to satisfy those curiosities and soothe any misgivings. Operational readiness is bigger than change management, bigger than communications, bigger than training. It encompasses all this—and more. In a nutshell, operational readiness means reaching out to every person who will be affected by the project you are sponsoring, and providing them with context, information, and training. It's a process that starts long before it's time to go live.

"But…" you might say, "We have a great training department! We're good to go."

Unfortunately, that isn't good enough. Excellent training is a crucial component of operational readiness, and the work done by your training team is indispensable to the process (as I'll discuss later in this chapter). But there's more. When employees are trained, they're taught to use the new process or system. When employees are led through the process of operational readiness, they're provided with the full picture: they're trained, *and* they're given the professional and emotional support they need to become comfortable with all the ways the new project will affect not only them, but their colleagues, vendors, clients, and so forth.

Think about it this way: Say you want to move to a new house, and you enlist my help. In January, I tell you: "Hey, we're going to be moving you to that new house in June." You've been wanting this new house, so you and your family are excited at the prospect, but still—it's a big change; one that will significantly affect your life. In this scenario, "operational readiness" would entail…looking at the house, having it appraised, making sure that the movers are lined up and the lights will be turned on, packing the boxes, and driving yourself over to your new home. It's a step-by-step process that unfolds comfortably over the course of months.

"Training," on the other hand, would be the equivalent of…when June rolls around, I pick you up at your old house, and I drive you over to your new house across town. I give you the key, shake your hand, and away I go.

In theory, the end result is the same in either case: *you are now living in a new house.* But the latter experience—being plopped in without any preparation—would be a bit jarring, don't you think? In the "training" scenario, you spent six months—from January to June—knowing that a big change was coming, but having little information otherwise. It's only natural to presume that was a stressful six months, full of questions and fears. Would the house have the features you were looking for? Would the neighborhood be nice? No one could blame you if you spent those six months on tenterhooks, anxiously awaiting the big day. Well, this period of anxious waiting is exactly what your employees, vendors, and customers experience when a new project or system goes live without operational readiness. They're dropped into a new environment, one that will affect them every day from there on out. This can result in confusion, as well as a loss of productivity or money. In some extreme cases, the entire project has to be rolled back.

Human beings need support around change. For example, I worked as a project manager for an aerospace and defense corporation, and was in charge of managing Y2K (turn of the century) readiness. There was a lot of angst in the company about Y2K, as you can imagine, so we made it our goal to prepare the technology *and* the people—and maybe even have some fun with it, if you can believe it. So, we did an M&M's theme (they had printed "MM"—the roman numeral for two thousand—on their candies in celebration of the new millennium). We rented out the local cinema, gave away candy and treats, and gave presentations telling people what they could expect. We followed up with information, training, and team involvement in the testing of changes. In the end, it felt like a non-event. We were well prepared, the changes went smoothly, the team was ready, and we all went about our business as usual. The operational readiness effort was crucial to the comfort and security of those people who were affected by the changes made to accommodate the new century. In many instances, the change itself is less troubling than the *anticipation* of change. Operational readiness helps make that anticipation as painless as possible, and, in the case of the M&M's, even fun.

...

Sam stopped by the accounts payable department to talk to their director. "Benjamin, I have a job for you," he said.

Benjamin groaned. "What is it—delivering some sort of bad news? Has something gone wrong?"

"No! What makes you think that?"

"I just like to keep my expectations low," Benjamin said wryly. "That way, I'm never disappointed."

"Well, aren't you a ray of sunshine," Sam said. "But, no—things are going great!"

Benjamin looked skeptical. "Yeah, right. The last project was 'great,' too, and we all know how that turned out." Sam couldn't blame him for his attitude; Benjamin was good friends with the head of customer service, who was still fielding complaints.

"We've been trying some new strategies this time around, and it's actually been going smoothly. We're on schedule, the quality is where it needs to be, and morale is high."

"So, what do you need me for?"

"Since your team is going to have to live with the new system once it goes live, I'd like you to be the point person for our operational readiness efforts," Sam said.

"Operational readiness?" Benjamin gave him a quizzical look. "Don't we have a training department? What do you need me for?"

"Yep, we have an excellent training department," Sam said, "and you'll be working with them, too. But operational readiness is bigger than training. And trust me, it's going to make your life easier in the end."

"Well, I do like 'easier'…" Benjamin said, gesturing for Sam to take a seat. "Tell me what I need to do."

…

Assigning a Point Person for Operational Readiness

Your operational readiness efforts are going to require a point person. Ideally, this should be the business leader who will live with the new system or process after it goes live. That's why Sam chose the director of accounts payable, since his people will live with the outcome of the project. The point person should ask questions and make sure that everyone is informed and that their risks and fears are addressed. The goal is to consider each and every facet, each and every person who will be affected—this can include customers, vendors, and other business partners—and help smooth their transition.

There are no hard and fast rules for achieving operational readiness, but these are some good general questions for your point person to start with:

- Which areas will be affected by this change? Who are the people in those areas?

- Are the processes defined as-is and in the new state?

- Which systems will be affected? If new systems are being installed, is there a clear plan for user testing and implementation, including a plan to retire old systems?

The operational readiness point person will first want to talk to the managers of the affected areas, to get them on board and explain why the project has been undertaken and how it will benefit the business (including the customers, if they are directly affected). Then, the point person and the managers can work together to craft a plan for handling the upcoming change. It's very important that this change is co-managed; managers should be part of the discussion and should help craft the messages that are then shared with the employees in their groups. Managers know their people, and can help identify which employees hate change, which ones are natural leaders, and which are early adopters. Of course, these different personality types should be treated differently. For those who hate change, work on them first and get them feeling comfortable. Likewise, get the early adopters fired up as soon as possible so that they'll evangelize to their coworkers. This way, it's not a matter of "making" people understand the change; it's a matter of bringing them in as partners in implementing these changes as painlessly as possible.

Sometimes, the fact is, new systems can create efficiencies that reduce the number of employees needed. Though this may be beneficial to the business as a whole, it creates an understandably unhappy situation for those managers who might have to lay people off, and for those employees who live in fear of being laid off. A crucial part of operational readiness is figuring out how to deal with that reduced head count. Address this early on and be as transparent about it as possible, or else your best performers will quickly find new jobs and the remaining folks will be paranoid and fearful, waiting for the ax to fall. As a sponsor, it's very important that you engage your human resources department early and figure out a plan for either finding new positions for folks or laying them off.

Where Training Fits In…

Training is certainly a part of operational readiness, but it's too frequently treated as the end all, be all. Obviously, when a new process or product is introduced, people need to be trained in how to use it. But if your organization hasn't undertaken a true operational readiness effort in the past, you might find your training department offended when you initiate a more comprehensive process. The training department may see this change as a message that their own work has been deemed "not good enough." If this is the case, please take the time to get your training department on board and encourage them to see how a more holistic operational readiness effort will actually benefit them as trainers. After all, their job is to know the new system inside out and create training tools that get employees familiar with the layout and features of that system. Training is actually more difficult when employees are distracted by their anxieties and other emotional baggage that comes with poorly managed change. Operational readiness supports and enhances the training process, and hopefully makes life easier for those conducting the training.

Operational Readiness and the Financial Big Picture

When it comes to your operational readiness efforts, don't get seduced by the allure of short-term savings. Businesses are always looking for ways to maximize their profits and cut expenses. This is perfectly understandable, but it can also lead to illogical cost-cutting that benefits the present at the expense of the future. I encourage you to view operational readiness not as an expense, but as an investment in the company's long-term health. The benefits are many:

- Minimize disruption to productivity
- Maximize comfort and awareness around the change
- Create company-wide understanding of the business benefit of the new project

"Comfort" and "understanding" may seem like intangible benefits, but they show themselves in tangible financial ways, and if they're absent, the bottom line will suffer. There's a saying that "It's better to pay the grocer than to pay the doctor." Meaning, you can pay *now* to prevent disease, or you can pay *later* to cure it. But, like it or not—you will pay, and it usually costs less to prevent a problem than to fix it. This saying holds true in business, too, especially when it comes to project management. Corners that are cut in the short term will undoubtedly cut you back in the future. If a project is pushed through without sufficient attention to operational readiness, it will undoubtedly have an adverse effect when the project goes live and time, money, and productivity are lost, and employee morale and customer satisfaction suffer.

How You as a Sponsor Can Support Operational Readiness

To support operational readiness in your organization, the first step is to make sure that an operational readiness plan is in place, and that your point person understands its importance and is fully committed to seeing it through. And, of course, always ask, "How can I help?" With your bird's-eye view of the entire project, you're in the best position to know just how many people—within the company and outside—will be affected by the change. With your influence, you can serve as a vital link between those many people.

If you want to really cross all of your T's and dot all of your I's, you can require that your operational readiness point person collect a signed attestation from every affected employee. This is a document that states something to the effect of "I attest that I have been trained and feel ready to implement the new system." That way, you know that no one will be surprised. This might seem like an overly formal step, but it's worthwhile to make the time to do this, as it gives you the security of knowing that no one has been overlooked. Or, if someone *has* been overlooked, this attestation gives them the opportunity to speak up and get their questions or concerns addressed.

...

"Well, I have to hand it to you, Sam," Benjamin said. "You were right."

Sam smiled broadly. "I was right? I like conversations that start this way."

"I admit I was skeptical about this whole 'operational readiness' thing when you approached me, but…it's been a real eye-opener."

"How so?"

"I just had no idea how deep the worries would go. Me, I'm like, 'New system. No big deal.'"

Sam laughed, not at all surprised by Benjamin's low-key attitude. Benjamin was definitely a technology enthusiast; he was always first in line for the latest gadgets and apps. A new system would be no problem for *him*. "You didn't say that to your people, I hope…"

"I admit, there were times when I wanted to," Benjamin said with a laugh. "But, no, I did exactly what you asked me to, and folks seemed to really appreciate it. Most seemed to find it comforting that all of their concerns were being logged and accounted for, and that I was connecting the dots between the various departments that'll be affected by the new system."

"It sounds like you were able to create a sense of cohesion for people."

"Exactly," Benjamin said, snapping his fingers. "Like, all parts are present and accounted for. Whereas, in the past, it always seemed like the right hand didn't know what the left hand was doing."

"Well, that's great. Is there anything you need from me?"

"Nope." Benjamin shook his head confidently. "I have a few concerns left to deal with, and then all that's left will be the attestations. Then we'll be good to go."

"I'm really impressed, Benjamin."

"Well, hey, thanks for asking me to take point on this. It's actually been fun, getting to talk to people and bringing them on board."

Sam watched Benjamin walk away, amazed that this was the same skeptical guy from just a couple months back.

…

Critical Thinking Questions

- Is there a small part of my brain that thinks operational readiness is a problem for human resources or some other department? If so, how can I reframe my thinking to see how I, as the sponsor, can offer great value in this endeavor?

- Do I take ownership of my responsibility to "inspect what I expect" when it comes to the operational readiness of the organization, customers, vendors, and business partners? Have I inspected the results of the work I asked my people to perform?

- What is my gut telling me? Am I confident that the organization is ready?

Chapter 7
Going Live…and Beyond

After months of hard work, the finish line is in sight, and you and your team are pressing ever closer to what will hopefully be a successful go-live. In this chapter, I break down the final sequence of events that will help you take your project live—and beyond.

Starting with the Cutover Plan

The cutover plan details the sequence of events that make up the go-live process. This plan is very in-depth, oftentimes broken down to the *minute* if the project is highly technical. However, despite the fact that this is a crucial document that keeps every team member on track during a critical process, I am always surprised when a cutover plan doesn't exist. This means that either the organization doesn't see the value in creating one, or the project manager and team are too busy to stop and make one, which is likely to happen if they're scrambling to finish tasks and complete milestones under pressure of a too-tight deadline.

Whatever the case may be, I encourage you to require a cutover plan from your project manager. It should be a document wholly separate from the project plan. The project plan will refer to the cutover plan; it will include "finalize cutover plan" as a milestone and include checkpoints at ninety days, sixty days, thirty days, and two weeks prior to the go-live event. But the project plan and cutover plan are two separate documents. A great cutover plan includes:

- Statement of the project purpose
- Project success criteria
- Names and phone numbers (including home or mobile) of all personnel involved in cutover
- The names and phone numbers of the management and sponsors who will be involved in cutover or will be available for escalation if an issue arises
- Minute-by-minute schedule of events
- Communication plan for the night of cutover, including milestone conference calls
- Risk assessment, stating any new risks that may have been identified in the process of putting together the cutover plan
- Emergency process
- Backout plan

Reviewing the Cutover Plan

The project manager should finalize the cutover plan no later than thirty days before the go-live event. This should not be a last-minute document, as you need time to review it thoroughly, and the project manager needs time to make any revisions based on your feedback.

If the cutover plan is missing any of the must-have elements listed above, send it back to your project manager. If you have any questions, be sure to ask them. As the guardian of the project, you are ultimately responsible for the success of the cutover, and it's better to ask questions early so that your team isn't attempting to answer them when it's crunch time. Be sure to ask your project manager:

- Who was involved in putting this cutover plan together?
- How confident are you in terms of the plan's quality and accuracy of it?
- How risky is the cutover? Were any new risks identified during the planning process?

...

Sam paced his office, thinking through all of the worst-case scenarios that could potentially befall the night of go-live. He had the cutover plan in hand, and had read it front to back. It was very thorough; he definitely had to give Sarah credit for that. She seemed to have thought through all of the critical components: personnel, milestones, conference calls, risks… everything seemed to be present and accounted for. Even though the project was big, and risks still lingered, Sam felt more confident than he had before any go-live that he could remember. He and his team had been so diligent up till now, Sam knew they could handle any scenario that came up.

But still, he wanted to be thorough in his review. It was better to consider all the angles now than to expect his brain to function if Sarah called him with some emergency in the middle of the night. The only bit that seemed not quite right was the minute-by-minute schedule of tasks. The list was thorough, but it was presented as a long list of bullets, and some of the tasks seemed to be out of order. He could see that causing confusion. Was that too nitpicky? Should he just let it go? But, he figured, it would only take two minutes to jot a quick email to Sarah. He sat down at his keyboard:

Sarah, the cutover plan looks great. My only concern is the list of tasks; they're not listed in order of when they'll happen. Can you reorder that—and use a numbered list rather than bullet points? I think that'll make it easier for people to follow along. Other than that, I think we're good to go. Thanks for all your hard work.

A minute later, his email pinged. *Thanks, Sam! I don't know how I could have missed that. Thanks for the heads-up. I'll definitely reorder that list and number it.*

Whew. Sam picked up the cutover plan and perused it one last time. But it seemed otherwise airtight. Barring an act of God, it looked like this cutover might just go off without a hitch, Sam thought with a smile.

...

The Sponsor's Role During Cutover

As the project sponsor, your role in the cutover is to

- Ensure that key players are on-call to support the team members

- Be sure there is a plan for assessing risks, issues, and emergencies as they arise

- Be ready to make on-the-spot decisions as needed

Though you do not need to be present for every moment of cutover, it's crucial that you're at least readily available by phone or email. If you are absent from this process, the whole thing can go south, because the team might be too fearful to push a project live if troubles arise and there's no decision-maker there to tell them how to handle it.

Communication During Cutover

Communication is an indispensable element of a cutover process. There should be conference calls throughout the process—four or five calls at predetermined milestone points, as outlined in the cutover plan. These calls do not need to be exhaustive; they can be brief, but do they do need to happen. If the go-live takes place overnight, there should be conference bridges held throughout the night. In addition to the conference calls, the project manager should issue an hourly report via email to all interested parties. It's vital that, from start to finish, communications are consistent.

What Happens in an Emergency?

Inevitably, at about 2:00 AM, some emergency situation is going to crop up. You can almost set your watch by it.

That's why the cutover plan should include an emergency process. Of course you can't always anticipate every problem that will arise, but you can be as prepared as possible by implementing an emergency protocol.

When an emergency situation occurs, the project manager will call you to apprise you of the situation. He or she will most likely be able to recommend a course of action, but it's up to you to decide. You need to ask, "What are the options—go forward with a defect, delay, back out?" and "What are the ramifications for that option—and is it an acceptable ramification?" Be sure your business lead is involved and can speak to the options. You may choose to go forward, you may choose to back out. Some of the problems may have already been identified in the risk list; hypothetical emergency scenarios should have been identified—and hypothetically solved. So, because the project manager, business lead, project team, and you, their fearless leader, have been ruthless in identifying and planning for emergency scenarios, these will not come as a surprise to you, and you won't have to depend on your brain to be working optimally at two o'clock in the morning. You'll be making an on-the-spot decision, but it will be a fully informed decision that was, ideally, thought through months in advance.

Crossing the Finish Line (Hopefully)

Cutover results in one of three outcomes: (1) You successfully go live with no problems; (2) you go live with a problem that you have agreed to go live with; or (3) the cutover fails and you have to back out and go live at a future date. Obviously the first option is ideal, but no matter what happens, it shouldn't be a surprise to anyone involved. With excellent communication, all key people were kept informed as the process unfolded.

•••

The team was gathered for the cutover. They were just moments from beginning, and Sam could tell that spirits were high and people were feeling confident. There was a noticeable lack of the panic and pessimism that accompanied other cutovers. Instead, there was an alert, engaged energy in the room, and everyone seemed to be on-point with what was expected of them and how cutover would progress. Sam wondered if this is what it felt like to be the coach of a team that was just about to head into a big game. He was there to motivate and direct as needed, but knew that the players—the ones out on the field, really making it happen—were as ready as they'd be. They'd practiced hard and were ready to play. Sam felt a sudden urge to dump a bucket of Gatorade on someone.

"We're ready to get started," Sarah said, interrupting his reverie. "It's time to kick off with our first conference call."

And with that, they were off. For the most part, Sam sat back and watched the team work their way methodically through the cutover plan, occasionally fielding questions that came his way. At first he was on tenterhooks, waiting for one of those emergency scenarios to rear its ugly head. But the first milestone was reached, and then the next: "We've got all the vendors available in the new system," Sarah said happily. And a little later: "All the invoices have been copied over." It began to dawn on Sam that their hard work was paying off. The proof was right here!

"Sam, if you'd like to head home and get some sleep, you should feel free to. I've got your phone number—I can call if there's an emergency."

"Are you sure?" Sam asked. He was about to object, but when he opened his mouth, a huge yawn came out.

"Yes," Sarah said emphatically. "Get outta here."

Sam was glad to get home and get in bed. It would behoove him to be well-rested the next day, when program defects or training deficiencies were likely to show up. He put his cell phone on his nightstand, just in case...

The phone rang at 5:00 AM. It was Sarah. Sam jumped awake, his adrenaline pumping. "What's wrong?" He asked.

"Nothing at all," Sarah said. She sounded tired but happy. "The system is live! Cutover went off without a hitch."

Sam rubbed his eyes. "Is this a dream?"

"No," Sarah said, laughing. "But you can go back to sleep—you can read the full report in the morning."

...

Post Go-Live: Handling the Transition

Even with a successful cutover and go-live, there's still work to be done in the post go-live period. You and your team are almost done, but it's crucial to maintain momentum. As the sponsor, make sure you're getting regular updates during this transitional period. Get a report immediately after the project goes live—what went well, what didn't, and what needs to happen next—and be sure to review it. If any unexpected defects revealed themselves, be sure that the project manager has created a contingency plan for dealing with them.

Even with a successful project launch, there will be some aftermath that reveals bugs in the system or gaps in user training. To handle this post-launch transitional period—which should ideally take no more than 36 hours—you should make sure that a protocol is in place. This might be a "hot phone," where users can call and get immediate assistance. Or a "war room," where team members are dedicated to spending time logging bugs and defects, answering questions, troubleshooting problem, and updating training materials. Another good practice is to have a team ready to walk the floor during business hours to immediately be able to answer training questions and look for any defects that may have been undetected until the system was actually in production. Be ready to create on-the-spot job aids for the most frequently asked questions or defect work-arounds as needed.

Similarly to the cutover process, the post go-live process requires that the project manager send the same frequent updates. This way, you'll always be aware of the number and types of problems and how they're being dealt with. In a poorly executed project, the war room can go on for weeks. Twenty-four to forty-eight hours is optimal, but the war-room phase can stretch to weeks and weeks when a subpar project is set live, because its downfalls will be immediately apparent to its users, and the cut corners will come back to haunt you. At some point, the number of issues should wind down, as bugs and defects are reported and fixed. Or, in a poorly executed project, you might just have to close the war room when it becomes apparent that nothing more can be done to improve upon the project. In either case, since you've been receiving regular updates, you can make an informed decision as to when to close down the war room and wrap up the post go-live period.

Lessons Learned

Once the dust has settled from the go-live and its immediate aftermath, you can sit down with your project manager and team, and come up with a list of lessons learned. This process is conducted similarly to the risk workshop, and led by the project manager. But in this case, the project team goes around the circle and offers their honest opinion on what went well and what they can do better next time. Discourage your project manager from asking "What did we do badly?" because that will lead the conversation down a path of blame and defensiveness. This workshop is not a place to mention names or place fault. What you want is a positive environment of honesty and growth, and the project manager should set that tone. Though, if you see that the conversation is going down a negative route, you should step in and redirect it.

Now, it's easy to ask people to be honest; it's much harder to give them genuine assurance that there will not be negative repercussions, and to genuinely hear their honest feedback and integrate it into future project sponsorship. Don't paint people as whiners or naysayers if they speak up. When you ask "What can we do better next time?" you give people the opportunity to work in an environment of growth rather than one of stagnation.

It's important that the lessons learned are used to improve future projects. If you ask for feedback and the same problems crop up persistently, never to be resolved, people will notice that, and they will learn that it's futile to articulate potential improvements if those improvements are never made. A good way to ensure that lessons learned are addressed next time is to require that your project manager feed those lessons learned into the risk list for the next project. That way, when a similar project is embarked upon, those newly discovered risks are right at the forefront.

Critical Thinking Questions

- Did I attend to the ninety-day, sixty-day, thirty-day, and two-week checkpoints before the go-live? Is my name, as well as the key people on my team, on the go/no-go decision with a confident YES?

- Did I delegate the critical checkpoint tasks to someone else more than once?

- Was I looking for the communications and available for the critical conference calls during go-live?

- Have I held my team accountable throughout the project so that the go-live is a well-executed event, or did it sneak up on everyone at some surprise date?

- Prior to go-live, was I in communication with my peers who will be taking over the operations of the project once it's launched?

- If the operations stayed in my area of responsibility, was my management team confident in their new world?

- Did the project meet the critical success factors outlined in the charter?

- Did I require that a "lessons learned" session was conducted, and did I review those results? How will I be sure that best practices and improvements called out will be in place for the next project?

Chapter 8
Recognizing Your Team

Sam sat back in his chair, smiling broadly after reading the project wrap-up that Sarah had just sent him, along with a note thanking him for his leadership. *Sam, this was the smoothest project I've ever managed. I can't believe we accomplished this great project—and under budget too! We couldn't have done this without you.* He could hardly believe how well it had gone, and it honestly hadn't taken him any more time or energy than past projects had. His boss had even taken him out to lunch to pick his brain about what Sam had done differently this time.

Sam picked up the phone and dialed his project manager. "Sarah! Good morning," he said.

"You sound happy," she said.

Sam felt like a proud father. "I couldn't be more pleased with how this project went off. I'd really like to treat the team."

"Really? There's a budget for that?"

"Why wouldn't there be?"

"Past sponsors have always told me we couldn't afford it."

Sam groaned, rubbing his forehead. He wondered how many times he himself had said there was "no budget" for celebration. Probably a few. Not this time, though. "How much would it cost to cater lunch for everyone?"

"A few hundred dollars."

"That seems reasonable. Do you have time to put together a party?"

"Oh, I'll make time," she said confidently. "This team worked so hard, I'd love the opportunity to celebrate. What day would work for you?"

"Me? Why me?"

"You have to come, Sam! You were a huge part of our success."

"I'm sure people don't want the boss around, spoiling their good time."

"Not true," she said emphatically. "If you don't come, people will think you only cared enough to pull out the company credit card. If you show up and give even a quick 'thank you' speech, people will know you're sincere."

Sam pulled out his calendar. It was packed pretty tight, but Sarah was right—he had to show up. "How about the 15th of next month?" he asked.

"Perfect," Sarah replied.

...

If you, like Sam, have never held a celebration for your project team, you're not alone. Celebration is typically not a facet of corporate culture. Usually, projects wind down and folks simply move on to the next item on their "to do" list. Plus, remember, as mentioned in the introduction, over 37 percent of projects fail. And even those that don't fail might be fraught with defects or don't meet the original scope. Perhaps the team is exhausted from a war room that dragged on for weeks as frustrated users found bug after bug. Depending on just how many unresolved problems were faced during the project, it may be that no one feels there's much worth celebrating.

Well, the good news is: once you begin implementing the simple strategies I've outlined in this book, you'll have something to celebrate. When your projects are a source of pride, it'll be only natural that folks will want to gather and celebrate a job well done.

But…What If the Project Fails or Is Cancelled?

Before we break out the streamers and party hats, I want to acknowledge the reality that not all projects will see a successful conclusion. How you handle this will most likely depend on the circumstances. If the project failed because of negligence, you owe it to your organization and your people to do a review and get to the root cause of the problem. Make sure to do a "lessons learned" workshop so that these failures can be used as teaching tools, and therefore bring some value to the company—even if just to serve as cautionary tales. Also, and I know this is not pleasant to think about, but take a critical look at your own actions to see to what extent you played a part in the project failure.

Perhaps, through no one's fault, the project was cancelled for some reason, such as a change in funding, direction, and so on. Or perhaps your team is as hardworking and diligent as can be, but the scope of work just simply wasn't achievable given the timeframe they were handed. If either of these two situations is the case, the team deserves to be acknowledged for their hard work.

Celebrating Success

Now, if the go-live went well and the project is by all accounts a success, it's definitely time to celebrate. Though it's easy to see this as an expense, I encourage you to instead see it as an investment in the *next* project. When you sincerely recognize and commend your team for a job well done, they will remember—and they'll want to deliver for you during the next project. The truth is, your team will work harder for recognition than they will for pay. Of course, they need the pay, too, but the recognition makes a big difference in the level of passion and creativity they bring to their work.

Just as I spoke earlier of the need to be forthcoming with mistakes and concerns, it's important to be just as generous—if not more so—with sincere praise and recognition. When you affirm your team members' strengths, you bolster their sense of worth, both to themselves and to the organization. This will help you retain your best talent and build a group of high achievers who can be counted on to help you meet your goals. Plus, if you create a place where people feel valued, it also becomes a place where they feel comfortable being open about their weaknesses and mistakes rather than finding ways to justify or offset the blame elsewhere. This means that you can count on them to be honest when your project manager asks them what keeps them up at night. It means that, when they make mistakes (which we all do), they'll own up to them and be diligent in seeking solutions—rather than papering them over.

There are easy ways to provide recognition that will have an emotional impact. You can send each team member a personal email, thanking them for their particular contribution to the project. You can have a creative administrative assistant put together a personalized certificate for each team member—signed by you, of course. Your project manager can organize a catered lunch or dinner, at which you can give an in-person "thank you" to the whole team. Or better yet, do all of the above. The key takeaway, though, is that you should make the effort to show your sincere personal appreciation.

Critical Thinking Questions

- Did I recognize my team personally and thank them for their hard work?

- If the project failed, did I take a hard look at the reasons? What could I do better next time?

- If the project was successful, how do I plan to bring those successes into the next project?

Conclusion

Beyond This Book...

Before we wrap up, I have one last critical thinking question for you to consider: *What will you take away from this book?* I hope you'll pause here and spend a moment to really think about that before you close the covers (or turn off your e-reader). Maybe even jot down some notes about how you can implement the strategies we've explored here. No matter how successfully your organization handles its projects, there is undoubtedly room for improvement. My hope is that you've gained some insights that you'll be able to parlay into bottom-line benefits.

Great project sponsors combine the right *attitude* with the right *actions* at the right *times*. This holds true across all industries, companies, projects, and methodologies. If you keep in mind these essential takeaways, *you* can be that great sponsor:

- Cultivate integrity within yourself and within your organization.

- Build trusting relationships with your team members.

- "Inspect what you expect."

- Ask questions and follow up.

- Create effective accountability systems.

- Recognize your employees and celebrate success.

Thanks for reading, and here's wishing you the best of luck with your future projects.

Acknowledgments

I'm grateful for all those who contributed to the creation of this book. Thank you to my co-author Sheila Ashdown, publisher Suzanne Chiles of Fresh Ink Foundry, and designer Joseph Loveria; to Glenn Ohl, Hussein "Sam" Hashem, and Peggy Wiley for their valuable feedback. Also thanks to my family, friends, and my husband, Perry Carbone; and to my Lord Jesus Christ. I appreciate your support and encouragement.

About the Authors

Terri Carbone

Terri Carbone is a dynamic, forward-thinking manager with more than twenty-five years of experience delivering successful projects and programs across a range of business sectors, including technology, healthcare, and aerospace and defense. Find her online at www.successfulprojectsponsorship.com.

Sheila Ashdown is a freelance writer and editor based in Portland, Oregon. Find her online at www.sheilaashdown.com.

www.ingramcontent.com/pod-product-compliance
Lightning Source LLC
Chambersburg PA
CBHW051814170526
45167CB00005B/2004